God's Hands: Beacon of a Pariah

God's Hands: Beacon of a Pariah

Robert Cooper

Urban Publishing House LLC

CONTENTS

CONTENTS

Prison exhales a mingled odor of freedom and misery. And on these plantations, a fortune of hope can be confiscated without warning, most times ending upon irretrievable loss.

The charges that brought me to these confines were convoluted, and with so many flying pieces and parts, it would have taken me digging up Johnny Cochran to sort out the mess of angles investigators used in order to build a case against me (which wasn't a tall order, being that I'm poor, black, and in the state of Texas). I recognized early on in the trial that I was being represented by an insufficient counselor, and this revelation left me contemplating a plea for a downward departure in sentencing during recess.

Pleading for fifteen years didn't leave me feeling accommodated at all, in fact, I felt cheated. And although over a period of time, I learned the importance of loving myself and smiling; I also developed a quiet anger toward this judicial system so intense you could walk up and touch it... I equated it to the kind of rage produced by a whip racing against black flesh bound in heavy chains.

But unlike most men plagued with this emotional erosion, I refused to allow it to consume me whole. Instead, I buried anger deep inside my conscience soil. Today I'm amazed at its Poetic Solace; I marvel at how my decision to compress anger is now producing healthy thoughts and meaningful conversations.

"My comrades, you are stronger than these powers which have an invested interest in seeing you render yourself a loser, and forever mad at the world. We are winners!"

Moreover, we are God's sinners; and by acknowledging so, we take away the power of man who throws stones at our existence or orchestrates through public opinion a stage for our demise. I implore each and every one of you to work diligently on forgiving and finding peace amidst the fury. This task will be challenging, but when it comes to rising to the occasion, you and I are well-to-do men.

"My comrades, do not let the sun go down on your anger; there is calm in being a passive traveler... And should you need a smile to help you along the way- You can have one of mine."

Written By Pariah/RC

The day I met Pariah, I was high. Yeah, I was high as a Kite! I remembered leaning up against the wall of a South Dallas Corner Store Called "Little World." When he approached me and asked, "Where the green at?" I replied with, "Who are you?" He smiled, that big bright smile of his, and said, "I'm Boomone or Pariah, depending on the day."

"So, you ain't the police?"

He raised his right pants leg up and asked, "Would a police be wearing one of these?"

On his ankle rested a monitor. I ended up selling him, let's just call it, a $20^{00} bag of medical Marijuana. He rolled up the fattest blunt I'd ever seen. Afterward, he broke it in half and gave me one. Halfway through our smoking session, he asked if I had ever heard Spoken Word before.

Of course, I hadn't, but I told him I had. I lied.

"Check this out," he said.

What I heard him do with dem' words was mind-blowing! The passion he displayed gave me chills and brought tears to my eyes. For real . . . I'm not playing. After he finished, he asked if was I ok. To be honest, at that moment I started to feel like a wimp sitting there with $500.00 worth of Dro, and a 45 pistol on me, getting emotional in front of a stranger. I guess it is true, that words, too, can soothe the savaged beast. Since that day up at Little World, Pariah and I have become good friends.

In my time of hustling, I've come across many street cats; and for the most part, they all wore a previously recognized or described character, but I didn't get that same impression about Pariah. The dude was different, reserved, and slow to speak, which I now understand is what gives way to that mystic aura about him. I was recently on the phone with Pariah, and I told him about my plans to record a poetry album. He chuckled (I imagined him smiling on the other end of the phone).

"Well make sure you record it the hood' way."

"Why?" I asked.

"Because traditional poetry is a dying dinosaur, waiting for someone to pull the plug on it."

I said to myself, "There he go with dem' words again."

- Raymond Denwick, Jr.

ISBN: Paperback - 978-1-0882-8912-9

First Published By Urban Publishing House, LLC 2023
"Authors Who Write with Integrity, Intelligence, and Inspiration!"

Robert's Landing Page - urbanpublishinghouse.com/pariah
Company Email: admin@urbanpublishinghouse.com
Company Phone: 1-888-671-2922 (Ext. 101)
Company Web: urbanpublishinghouse.com

"GODHANDS"

I've witnessed pen and paper save souls;
And my expression became a gift,
Even when my action wasn't holy.
With a past dirty as mine, to man, it didn't make sense,
That I would want to save lives, and re-invent.

I can't invent perfection! What I own is my experience.
So I jot those down on paper,
And hope dear readers might learn from them;
And see the benefits and not my sins.

The world can judge the man,
But these are Godhands.

In good times, let me not become a stranger,
To the angels on the mountain.
What I am, is a writer,
Inspiring readers to become leaders with wide eyes,
Even I have expressed pro-found behavior,
And walked away with a closed mind.

Troubled . . . Waters . . . . Deep!
It feels like I'm walking on water every time Jesus weep.
If we're Jesus' people, why can't we find Jesus' peace?
What good is freedom when it leads,
To broken-bodied dreams, more guns, more violence,
More problems, more broken glass in the street,
Holding up broken bodies?

We can't change fate, With faith, we pray for God's favor;
We, God's children, sinners rightfully made.
Life is Crazy. Asylum crazies, try hanging themselves,
But the toilet paper keeps breaking.
"One" looked upon the wall and read my words:
This to shall pass-hold "ya" head!

Through Godhands,
I've touched and changed the heart of a dead man
Even though that same man, would pay to see my life end.
I can't walk on water. I'm not perfect; that's life.
This is not a speculative reality.
I can't walk on water Lord, at times, my hand feels tied;
It ain't easy trying to keep my head above the tide.
As I walk through the valley past the shadows in the dark,
Guide my way, place that radiant light in my heart.

"Godhands"

Written By, Robert Cooper

"BLACKFLAMES"

"Because I'm black," I get mad quick!
"Cause I'm black," I got bad kids.
"Because I'm black," they'll be born with animal inclinations,
And too ignorant to know what their worth is.

I just painted racism. Radical: "They attach this to me,
When I just want what's right for me and my people.
Though fate and free will are fondly related,
I'm seen as an extremist when I operate as a Free-Agent."

These Prejudgments not only come from the White race;
Black judges use the same measuring stick,
When sentencing our children to rot in cages.
Dreamers died for our freedoms;
Though we shouldn't settle down into this belief that we're Free.
And we shouldn't allow hate to shake our Faith,
But with undisturbed repose reclaim our place.

"Jesus wept, the day we lost our way."
Though, it all happens for a reason,
It would be defeating, if we start believing we only evolve for a season.

It's my responsibility to educate and communicate this to my seed;
Less I be like Grandaddy, "Rollin" over in his grave,
Ashamed and frustrated, at me and my people.

We deserve better than prison, and a troubled conscience.
We deserve better than inevitable consequence,
That put me in bed with my monsters.
Since I'm black, I belong on a short leash.
"Cause I'm black, the way I communicate frightens the police."
Because I'm black, time is not on my side;
These communist delusions make it easy,
For those who don't read to believe,
That me and my people will never rise.

I'm a victim, but there's no time to
Sit and wish for some mystic redemption;
We gotta man-up, and put some work in.
I'm a victim, but I'm a predator;
In the sense that I've hurt my brother,
Even when I held from Him knowledge,
My transgression was no lesser than canes murder.

"Blackflames"

Written By: Robert Cooper

"UKRAINE'S MANICURED IRONY"

SPOKEN WORD

The antique alarm clock sits on my mahogany dresser,
And, by its ancient sudden sound, I am awakened, feeling relaxed.
I could see from my pillow that the sky,
Is blue and pretty, and the sun was a bright one.
After a few minutes of taking in my morning fortunes,
I rosed from my bed,
And slowly made my way through the narrow hallway,
And there, near the living room entrance, I noticed the cat;
The one belonging to my ex . . .
The cat she has promised to retrieve, but never.

Unfortunately, when it came to being responsible, she was never that.
I assumed this was the way most narcissistic people treated their pets;
I considered the cat to be my own, now.
As I sat on the couch, it leaped up and took its place in my lap,
Purring and staring at the television,
While I fumbled about searching the cushion for the remote.
And with the remote in hand,
I casually began flipping through the channels,
(Barely interested in anything),

Then, reluctantly settled on the news.
Surprisingly Fox.

The volume is low, my coffee is black,
And from my checkered color cup, I took a sip,
And focused in on the reporter with a foreign accent,
And small lips saying:
"Ukraine is being attacked by the Russians!"
Her tone seemed a cautious climax . . .
Although scenes of Russian invasion appeared disturbing enough,
I emotionally disconnected from the Ukrainian's situation,
Since there were no black people in Kyiv,
Then, at the very end of that thought, images appeared on the Screen,
Of Africans waiting at the railway station in Kviv trying to flee.

Surprised, I should not be . . .
The racism in Poland ain't no different than racism on our shores,
Bleeding inland and placing burdens on our shoulders.
So what, if the Russians are coming, and they're taking land?!
American Indians are psychologically bombed,
"Because they cannot go back to theirs."
Indifferent, I sit with my thoughts suspended in the air.
I recalled when Rwandans were being slaughtered,
NATO didn't give a dam!
Ukraine, Ukraine . . .
I am ashamed that I'm not pained that bombs are raining.
I guess, I'm numb to the war,
Since in the Tulsa massacre, not even one angel came.

And in my lap napping is the cat; as black as me, and abandoned,
Seemingly we're perfect strangers . . .
I thought: "We're going to be alright," as I caressed him.
At least for now, we are not stranded at the border,

Or sitting bombed like those poor Ukrainians.

War is such an awful scene.
"But there's no nation of people whose situation is perfect."
And with this attitude, I embrace the ironic angles of my pen,
Along with the poetic cluster of satisfaction that engulfs me,
Whenever the ink runs and smears the paper,
Making room for my imperfections,
And giving way to the pros and cons of incorrectness,
While profoundly showing . . .
That everything in life is not simply wrong or right!

Some things are an abstract Black – like -I and the cat;
And others a daunting White.

"Ukraine's Manicured Irony"

Written By: Pariah/RC

4

"A MOTHER'S PRAYER"

It's cloudy out . . . God give my son direction.
He's been up and down life mountains,
And he still don't know his purpose.
I hope I'm not asking for too much, since I haven't been perfect,
But for all intent and purposes, sometimes I go to church.

Lord, like the morning sun, I hope Jesus finds him in His grace,
and that He treats my son as precious,
And not define him by a race.

Give him a beautiful touch, let not Your presence be a faze.
You know his flesh is weak,
So, Jesus, walk with him all the way.

I'm down on my knees, Lord, embracing Your patience,
When life gets hard for me, I find refuge in Your mercy.

I know you're listening!
I feel Your Spirit's real.
The Pandemic has taken millions Lord,
It's been a long year.

It's gon' be a homeless winter . . .
Shield my Son from the cold.
Blessed is he whose work is holy,
But show this sinner your warmth.

Give my daughter a husband.
Give my son a wife.
Free someone of cancer.
Save an addict's life.

Free someone from prison,
Bless the man who gave them time . . .
"We're all God's children, though we don't always get it right."
My son's a pariah, whose heart reflects a brighter side.
Did the last prayer I sent for him, ever make it past the clouds?

I'm praying for you, now, to come into his life.
And I'll always keep sending them, and keeping hope alive!
I'm down on my knees Lord . . .

"A Mother's Prayer"

Written By: Pariah/RC

"POETIC BEGINNINGS"

My name is Robert, I was born in Shreveport, Louisiana. Growing up, I started out being raised by two parents, though. Unfortunately, in the course of time, this union simply dissolved. My mom and dad didn't get along well, which in itself, is an

understatement, but for this reason, my mother, my siblings, and I moved around a lot. From Louisiana to Arizona, Texas, then back to Louisiana.

I wouldn't say that we were a dysfunctional family, although like most families, we had our ups and downs. Now, looking back, I can't necessarily say that we were an unloved or unhappy family. Simply put, we were just poor . . . Dirt poor! But somehow my brothers, sisters, and I still found ways to make comedy out of it all . . . and laugh about our situation, we did! We would make fun of the rubber Flapjacks, the watered-down sugar syrup, and our pissy mattresses. And whoever pissed the bed that night would be the headliner for jokes, until the next bed-wetter took their stage.

I can't speak for my siblings, but being impoverished made me feel totally isolated from the rest of society. It was here, in this isolation, where I became most curious about the world, people, and where I discovered writing as an outlet.

I'll never forget, sitting there in class one day, when my English teacher, Miss Curry, openly instructed me to go to the principal's office, without giving me a reason for my trip. The day before, we had been given a writing assignment and were presented with a subject to write about. As I was heading to the principal's office, I began to rewind my mischievous tape to the past week. through my head.

I couldn't help but think, "Surely, I've done something wrong and forgotten about it! Man, could they have found my fingerprints on one of the eggshells from the eggs that Jerry Peterson and I had thrown at the band room door? Maybe they've raided my locker and found my stolen pack of Kool Cigarettes!"

I swear, just thinking about that made me want to skip the principal's office and walk straight home! Of course, that would be suicidal because momma would hear none of my excuses, and she would find the truth, just like she always did. Plus, I was smart enough not to "jump out of the pot, and into the frying pan!" So, like the brave heart I was, I knocked on the principal's door . . .

The booming voice that followed my knock rattled my bones and made my chest feel hollow. "Come in!" he said. So, I eased way in head first, taking in my surroundings as if I were waiting for the cops to jump out; I was even scared that the floor might cave in and take me straight to Hell! But nothing happened . . .

Still, Mr. Wallace's smile didn't make me feel any safer. Mr. Wallace was a big man! A really big, black, hairy man; with a long paddle, and he knew how to nurse a grudge! "Have a seat, son," H said. "And don't be nervous, you're not in any kind of trouble . . .This time."

I wanted to say, "Thank you," but didn't. Instead, I just tried to relax. Mr. Wallace immediately started up with the questioning . . . "Do you recall these two pieces of paper?" he said.

"Yes." I replied.

"Did you write this? The assignment, I mean."

"Yes, I did. Yesterday, in Miss Curry's class."

"Who helped you come up with the words for this?" he asked.

"No one, sir."

"Impressive." Mr. Wallace said, "Brilliant, in fact!"

"Son, do you want to become a writer, one day?"

"No," I responded quickly.

'Well, why not, son?"

"Because writing is hard, Mr. Wallace, and I'm only a 7th grader, who finds listening to music, hanging out with my friends, and playing with my dog more appealing, Sir."

Mr. Wallace said, "Son, appeal will not be feeding you. It'll likely be the most unattractive things in life that will allow you the opportunity to obtain goals.

I wanted to say, "Yeah, whatever." But again, I said nothing, and just stared into those piercing eyes and continued working on relaxing.

Then he asked me, "Can you tell me what poverty is?"

Sure of this one, I responded, an uncomfortable feeling of want."
Mr. Wallace smiled, and then abruptly asked me, "What is tomorrow?"

Again, without missing a beat, I said, "Today, not yet becoming."

Mr. Wallace looked at me long and hard, then spun his chair around and stood up to open his filing cabinet, and there it was . . . Staring me right in the face! That famous bite! The one that Jerry always managed to have the class laughing about, including our teacher, as he imitated the "bite" himself by pulling a wedgie into his butt! So, I smiled and giggled out loud, distracting Mr. Wallace to the point that he glanced back at me for a moment. Then he shook his head in puzzlement, and said, "You are weird, son, but very special."

And, with those words, he then leaned his large body over his desk and handed me two pads, one pen, one pencil, and then he said, "Stay out trouble . . . And no matter where life takes you, keep writing!" And with that, I was dismissed.

That day when I walked into Mr. Wallace's office changed my life. And though it didn't prevent me from making bad decisions, his seeing me as "special," as he put it, had validated my existence. His effort to notice my talent, and his encouragement helped reshape how I viewed people. And his acknowledgment of what I had the potential to become gave me hope every time I found myself beneath the rubble of life.

Thanks, Mr. Wallace. May you rest in peace. And by the way, I'm still writing.

"Poetic Beginnings"

Written By: Robert Cooper/Pariah

"HEAVEN HAS A QUEEN"

It was July, a boiling hot summer day. The place, Canfield Ark. The people, more country than a bag of beans! Momma thought moving here was good since living here meant we would be close to her sister and brother, and our granddaddy. Plus, the country provided a form of protection for the kids. You didn't have to worry about getting mugged, raped, or jumped in Canfield; and even if you were to witness a fight, there was about a 90% chance it would be relatives getting at each other. Then, the chances would be even greater that somebody was drunk!

I loved it though . . . all of it! The fresh air, the trees, the butterflies, and the grasshoppers, I loved it all. It was a very hot July, I was nine years old, and little did I know that it would be this sun-blistering day that I would meet the love of my life. Boy, she sure was pretty, and brown, and unlike the rest of the lot, she shied away from people, almost running away from them as if she couldn't trust anyone. While observing all of this, I saw a little bit of myself in her; and I told myself then that we had a future together. Although she was reluctant to come, I gently picked her up and named her, "Queen."

When I stepped into the house, I sat her down on the living room floor, and she immediately high-tailed it under the couch. My brothers, Alfred, and Stafflon, were excited and gave chase after Queen, but I begged them not to mess with her, and to leave her be. Of course, my sisters, May, and Sherry, took off to the back to tell Momma that I had brought a dog home, and that it was in the house, which was strictly against Momma's rules.

Queen must have sensed all of the coming commotions, and that, coupled with the preexisting stress and tension, caused her to leave a trail of urine from where I sat her down to where she hid under the couch. I could hear my mother and sisters coming from the back, so I dropped down to the floor to try and retrieve my Queen from her spot under the couch. Unfortunately, she was too far back for me to reach her, but as I looked up at my brothers, and they looked back down at me, we knew, without saying a single word, that we had to stick together on this one. We had us a dog, and if it meant begging or turning backflips to keep her, we were prepared to do just that!

Momma wasn't buying any of it, at first, and she went on about how my uncle shouldn't have allowed me to even pick out a puppy without her permission; but we kept on begging, "Please, Please!" until she finally relented and gave in. It was one of our happiest moments ever, though she would go on to say, "Not in this house; the dog stays outside!"

So, by nightfall, we had taken some wood, tin, nails, and a hammer, and built Queen a pen. Once it was finished, we filled it with dry brown pine leaves and padded it with an old wool blanket. We made sure that the bottom was tight, and that the pen height was high enough to keep out the coyotes and other big bad creatures of the night.

After that was finished, we left her with plenty of food and water and watched her until it was time for us to go in. The first month or so, I would wait until everyone was asleep, and then I would sneak out back to check on Queen and hand-fed her snacks. I felt like I owed her this loyalty, and plus, I wanted her to trust me completely, and never hesitate to come running to me whenever we met. It worked, slowly at first, but sure enough, Queen became a popular figure around our house, as well as among my closest relatives and friends. She used to tag along whenever we took walks to the store, and she even played "Chase" with us out in the fields.

"Heaven Has a Queen:

Written By: Pariah/Robert Cooper

"HERO"

As we wait on the minds of science, summon the will.
You got it, and I have it to give:
Those sunbeams of courage to our peers,
Every fighter deserves to live.

Witnessing my daddy struggle for breath, and suffering,
Was like watching me dying.
Those chemo sessions that we attended play back in my mind,
A haunted reminder.
This one thing Daddy told me keeps me strong:
"Son, don't ever give up on your own!"

That advice was bold. Though, behind his eyes,
I could see his tears, and rightfully so.
Every day given served to make him stronger,
Though defeating Cancer is much harder,
Than repairing a tapered soul.
For nothing else but for the battle, cry, and be made whole!
For nothing else but for the battle,
Look Cancer in the eye like a soldier!
For nothing else but for the battle, go down a fighter!

And wake up in Heaven a hero.

"Doc, before your tenure ends, can you bring us answer?"
You know, the one we're all pursuing in the fight against cancer . . .
Beneath the rubble of discovery, children's lives are being ruined,
Which gives off a faint contribution of all the scholars in the room.

I'm just saying, Eric's 10, confined to a bed, praying for God's hands,
Listening to annoying hospital beeping noise, missing his friends.
Those same friends looking in at a winner!
Beyond that window, he left so many winners.

For nothing else but for the battle, he cried once, but no more.
For nothing else but for the battle, he looked Cancer in the eye,
Like a soldier.
For nothing else but for the battle, he fought like a fighter,
And woke up in heaven a hero . . .
If, for nothing else but for the battle.

"Hero"

Written By: Pariah/ R.C.

"THE LONG WALK ACROSS THE AISLE"

ESSAY

Not long ago, my white friends and I felt comfortable enjoying one another's company. Being in their presence was truly a color-blind experience. And our concern, which we expressed for one another's well-being, seemed genuine and shined upon my soul like a ball of humanity light. Now, unfortunately, when I look into their eyes, it feels as if I'm staring into holes leading into dark caves. Undoubtedly, we've changed with time; and trust me, times are ill. The political environment that we live in is overwhelming. and toxic at best. And the attempts to distort our "King" dream are real and very frustrating. Recently, in a tense and withdrawn conversation with one of my friends, he asked, "What happened to us?" I responded with painful insecurities and confusion by saying, "You became white." "But you became black, too," he replied. This was serious sarcasm on both our parts. However, I don't, for one second, believe my friend is a racist. But because of the rhetoric coming from would-be leaders, he now feels he has a valid argument when it comes to nationalism, immigration, police brutality, and of all things . . . "Obamacare."

I do not share many of his views, though silently, I trust we both agree on this one thing, that our political climate SUCKS! This sentiment is not an attack on our flag, our national anthem, or our democracy by far. But it's worth noting, that it's sad how we have allowed this oppressive institution of Man to push us back across racially divided lines and render us cautious compassion. I'm proud to be an American. Moreover, I'm fortunate to be an occupant of this rich land, but the bigotry and injustice that has once again made itself openly prevalent in my country, is not of my own. On the Left and the Right, I watched many cling desperately to racially degenerating times. One would think, that at least the majority of us were past that stage of hate and rage, which consumed those in the past. No, we are not a perfect nation. And in a society based on material gain, power will eventually corrupt. But this should be when the resolve becomes "We the People" cultivating a heart big enough to share with the world its love: Understanding and compassion, regardless of our differences in opinion.

These times will be recorded. So, ask yourself, how do you wish to be remembered? Surely not as a voiceless coward, hiding in the shadows, admirably watching these politicians smear hate on our beautiful patterns. If only we could imagine how important all our existences matter to each other; how little, then, doubt can estrange us, how precious we become. Nobody wins when separation is so wide that we shout and can't hear one another speaking. We're stronger together, much stronger than the walls politicians prop up to divide us and suspend our hope. When my grandson and nephews become men, and look back at 2017, I want them to be proud that I humbly spoke out in defense of all humankind. At present, we're besieged with turmoil; though in my heart, there's a dream that despair will inherit our happiness. And we'll begin to appreciate even those we don't love, and there will be no Democrats, and there'll be no Republicans . . . Just us, and every moment an American.

"The Long Walk Across the Aisle"

Written By: Robert Cooper

"ABSTRACT DIALOGUE"

Life owns my breath. So, I give it my blessings.
Life: This unattachable shadow follows me like a crazed spectator.
Following me, farther away from the abyss,
And pushing me consciously before a full-length mirror.

When I look in the mirror in my eyes, I see something . . .
I see those bright colors throughout my struggles,
That painted me Perfect.
To deny them love would be to abandon myself!
Together, we're better, for better, or worse.

The mirror embraces my essence,
Even though Bible thumpers see my moral compass as a matted mess.
The mirror embraces my essence;
And before it I stand erected and not a shallow presence.

Mirror, mirror, on the wall, talk to me!
I'm not worried that certain topics might trigger unwanted memories.
We do not have to discuss my mental injuries,
And this is not a plea for your sympathy.

Mirror, thanks for having the courage to look back at me.
You are my equal and not a replica of my reality.
Without "You," I wouldn't have found "Me,"
Or could see dreams once I close my eyes and set my mind free.

"Abstract Dialogue"

Written By Pariah/RC

"THE ABOLITIONIST SOUP"

SPOKEN WORD

I picked the cotton . . .Yeah, I picked the cotton.
Then I came out the fields to eat, but the food was rotten!
I stood to protest, but the rest would not . . .
Though it was clearly visible. Flies in the pot.

Go it alone, and be made a martyr.
Resolve isn't hostage to a perilous lot.
Teardrops from a tier, let'em drop,
Lead the charge, and leave your mark on this plantation plot.

For justice: We'll have to suffer to give it birth.
Before the judicial system renders justice, they will act to kill us first.
I picked the cotton; the heat felt like a furnace death.
I hurt my back and found my medical resolution pursued.

Behind the bricks, there's love, peace, and drama's loud music.
Psychologically I'm damaged, I can show you the bruises.
I'm throwin' pencils and paper tantrums to spread the news,
I tried telling these brothas I seen flies in the soup.

God knows the truth . . . I stood up from the table and shouted:

FLIES IN THE SOUP! FREE US FROM THESE CAGES:
Y'ALL GO PICK THE COTTON, I'M TURNIN' THAT PAGE
Then, I thrust my fist into the air and was tossed to the pavement.

A liberty institution for my brethren is the movement . . .
The food is rotten in the pot, I saw flies in the soup.
Without us what the hell the cotton gon' do?
Where goes pic if we slaves don't move?

Abolitionist? To be, or not to be, is an act of war.
I kept telling these fools the food was spoiled.
Abolitionist for freedom is worth dying for;
So place a casket wrapped in plastic outside my psychic door.

"The Abolitionist Soup"

Written By: Pariah/Robert Cooper

"MADE MEN"

Today, I seen a man walk a straight line,
With calculated time and wrinkles on his face.
And in every wrinkle, I seen the diminishing of a menace,
And the precious time he wasted. I saw age . . .

But beneath that surface, I seen the page he turned,
And that chapter, which once held him captive,
Make way for a new one.

I seen how the society that he grew up in manipulated and used him;
Abused him, and it confused him,
When they viewed him as a nuisance.
But what do you do, when you're from the ghetto,
And by it heavily influenced?
You can't expect a soldier to defect, abandon his set,
And dance to the music.

I stared at his boots, and by the dust,
I revisited that back muddy country road he took.
This made him humble, though, inside his struggle,
A soar vanity had took root.

Considered ruthless, and worthless to the future, so he drifted,
Deeper into the darkness of his seclusion.

From where he's from, his skins perceived a gun.
There, he's like "Kunta," nigger come out with your hands high,
"Cause you ain't got room to run."
They've surrounded the house and placed a cop on every corner.
Then, finally shot black in his back,
And all he had in his backpack was "chewing gum."

Society tells us this is life, and that there's no need to cry.
In prison, every day, a boy dies;
And a man appears in the mirror,
As beautiful as a butterfly ready to rise;
With angels on both sides of his wings,
This morning I looked in the mirror Momma, and seen a man.

"A man who found refuge in the Bible."
After reading every verse of Genesis, Exodus, Leviticus, Numbers,
This gangsta still hasn't decided;
Whether to step forward and accept his past for what it was,
He regretted with every inch of himself,
That day he picked them colors up.

As an adolescent, he left paradox messages for help,
On juvenile hall walls.
While he slept, in the distance he could hear his mother's voice saying,
"Son you're black, you have reason to be proud;
Lace-up 'yo boots, stick 'yo chest out, and tilt 'yo head to the sky."

"Son, you're black! You have reason to be proud."
Show submission to the opposition,
And you'll be crushed by the thousand,

Out of a thousand, one survivor will emerge to follow,
Because of the power of your pen, you'll be made a martyr.

The mistake of my oppressor is:
They didn't see a man evolving. "It took a minute,"
But I eventually looked in the mirror and seen a man Momma,
Kicking his heels against the wall;
As he sat on the edge unafraid of falling, to his death,
Till my death, I'll leave blood and sweat on these perilous mountains.

"Made Men"

Written By: Robert Cooper

"I CAN'T COMPLAIN"

I hear it all the time . . .
"Robert, you coulda' been somebody.
How did you get trapped in this situation,
When you shoulda' went somewhere?

Success was right there,
All you had to do was reach;
You coulda' had a grip on that little piece of mind called freedom.

The odds are fragile.
Why come you didn't beat them?"
I get it all the time . . .

"Robert, what is your plan now?"
Do you plan on tossing your pencil, pad, and your pen out,
And accepting a handout?

I know not you,
The guru, with your soul on pages?
Fo' sho' not you, the 'hustla',
With all that ink smeared on your apron?"

Haters can be so hateful,
but like them,
I have a job to do.
People talking down on me now,
Couldn't walk a mile in my shoes.

I can't complain,
True to myself,
And that's absolute.
A blessing going to come to a Hustla,
and that's absolute.

I'm pushing fifty, looking live,
Like that Mercedes "Poppa" shot at.
I thought that was "live,"
Until the windows came down,
Sending shots back!

At "Poppa" grave, I stood on top of dirt,
Looking into the heavens.

I can't complain,
Would it even matter?!

Nowadays I'm cautious.
All my losses,
I take with a grain of salt.
That's what a Boss do.

As long as "Momma" good,
And my grandson fed, I'm well.
I can spend a lifetime without worries in my prison cell.

Yes, I, the guru,
With my soul on pages.
All these smiling faces, have me pacing:
I don't know who is my hater.

Momma say, in my solitude,
I'll find answers to these questions;
And inside this solitary,
I'll begin to count my blessings.

And all that stressing, for nothing.,
Ain't going to change a thing.
I guess it is what it is then . . .

I can't complain.

"I Can't Complain"

Written By: Pariah/Robert Cooper

"IF I HAD LOVE"

Love,
Turn and walked out a slammed door!
So long ago that her face is a blur.
I've dreamt her back in my arms,
But chances are, she'll never return.

Love,
Rose from the ash of my failings!
Even in absence,

Love,
Is always and forever . . .
Always inspiring me to reach;
Reach out and touch love face,
Or place a kiss on her cheek.

Love,
Long I sought thee.
Oh, how I found, then lost you completely.
My lost is rich in pain and suffering;
My days are dark, and at night my heart clings to nothing!

But if I had love, she'd be the voice of my ideals;
My good fortune, and reason to live!
My motivation to rise strong and content;
My resolve, and ambition to dream!

If I had love,
I'd treat her more than some imaginary point in space . . .
I'd protect, and give love comfort when she hurt.
My trust in love would be as strong as my faith,
I'll honor and treasure

Love,
As if I'd mold her myself from clay.
If I had love . . .

"If I Had Love"

Written By Pariah/Robert Cooper

"Y'ALL LOOK SMALL FROM UP HERE"

I'm a diamond, shining. Beneath the soot in the pit.
Reluctantly confined to the dirt, Dreaming of being risen.
Hence, the man with no plan, Just a pan, and a wish;
Who found the will to emerge, and write his own ticket.

Limits and grudges, I grounded them up in the grit,
The genie in the battle, was just a delusion in the ashes.
Bring on the mountains: Challenges, are hard to resist.
It's either me, or my fears, to die a suffocated death.

So, I'll face them with confidence, every task, I swear.
Determination, and my words, are all I have in this world.
Because of my persistence, the tension, I can feel it in the air,
But I'm in the sky, so high, my apposition is a blur.

"Y'all Look Small from up Here"

Written By: Pariah/Robert Cooper

"LYING DOWN AND WAKING UP A SLAVE IN TEXAS"

SPOKEN WORD

It's Poetic . . .

In Texas, we're trapped in pits with small windows.
Inside these cells, we're funding our own imprisonment;
The chains are encrypted inside the chips and soup sales.
We're inside of an identity crisis, believing our soul out of favors,

So we accept the chains;
Believing a greater change will come save us . . .

Can you dis that?

I guess the Willie Lynch Syndrome dies hard in some places.
Since I'm older now, In these younger guys I see my own reflection.
It seems as if the hate for ourselves is baked in.
Perhaps it takes breaking one down,
In order to build one up and to make a man.

I used to beat up on myself!

The whipping took away my strength . . .
Then I killed my bad habits and drug'em to a ditch!
I changed from a threat to a promise;
But in Texas, I'll always be a number.
Every day it's the same old song . . .

In doubt: Our systematic scars found a home.
In Texas: It's death before parole.
In Unity: We can overcome!

But we won't . . .
Because by the throat, we're holding our resolve under the water.
Christians and Muslims accept this torture.
The trauma cemented the bangers in a corner,
Set-trippin', cooking drink, and getting stoned.

I envision us standing up for ourselves,
And not being exploited with little-to-no health care.
But tomorrow we'll be back in the "fields."
Under a sun giving off heat like Hell!

There ain't a Night I don't look beyond these walls,
With cataract eyes, and pull in the stars.
Today's a blessing . . . Every good one, I'll record them.
Tomorrow, I'll wake up a slave behind these bars.

"Lying Down and Waking up a Slave in Texas"

Written By: Pariah/Robert Cooper

"PRISON LIFE IS ABSTRACT"

SPOKEN WORD

No cell phones to download map apps.

One minute, you're happy; the next produces a large gap between happiness,

People, and situations you're at odds with.

The facts of prison life are cold to the touch.

You either hate those that turned their back on you,

Or, pray for love and their trust.

Every hour of the day creates an issue.

Life is unpredictable, waking up behind the bricks.

"But mind is the master."

Time shall be the pillar of resolve or wasted brain matter.

It's best I feast on the belly of the beast,

and get more out of it than it will get out of me . . .

"Prison Life Is Abstract"

Written By Pariah/RC

"BECOMING"

Life: Innocent as it's a four-letter word.

Love: More beautiful than the sun which shines on her.

Life and love:
It's not every day that we'll wake up with our heads high,
Put on make-up, and prepare to perform in their circus today.
In the pursuit of happiness, a new day we salute as winners.

The stars shouldn't shine if I'm not in them.
Oh, reader,
These words are shiny gates to a kingdom.

Oh, reader,
Believe! The sky is the limit, and life is unscripted.
Believe! The future needs your contribution.

Be reliant.
Don't be persuaded that being uncommitted has no consequence.
Uncommitment will make you dependent,
And mastered by small things.

You and I are giants!
Giants! When the water rises.
Giants! Cause we got the power to conquer, and not be devoured.
Come, unhappy isolated urban . . .
Come, American city dwellers . . .

Unmask so that we resemble "We the People."
Oh, reader,
These words are shiny gates to a kingdom:
We're the envy of diamonds;
Life may be unscripted, but we are defined.

"Becoming"

Written By Pariah/Robert Cooper

"FROM RAGS TO RICHES"

I'm trying to get from rags to riches,
Where it's all good; but in the past I've made some bad decisions.
To the point, that the means' which defined my 'end' are evil.
My daddy's gone, but Momma's still living;
And I don't want to lose her while I'm doing time in prison.
After surviving six penitentiaries, and a stint with religion,
Still, my heart is cold and empty.

Oh, reader, don't hold it against me because my soul is crippled,
And the road to riches is covered with debris, pins, and needles.
I'm a sinner, engulfed in bad decisions,
But like George Jefferson, going from good times,
I'm dreaming of the life of riches! Away
From scars, from bullets, to pads, and cushions;
From ashy elbows and ankles to living up in the high-rise angels.

Getting Street cash is lethal.
Since Elementary,
I've been on a mission to get from rags to riches.
If God created me after His own,
Then why is my image so blurry?
If it's He, who granted me free will,

Then why does it end so bloody?"
From rags to riches, not all my deeds are sins,
But Justice is not equal,
So still, I'll be judged a man . . .
From rags to riches . . .

"Rags to Riches"

Written By Pariah/RC

"THAT INVISIBLE DOOR"

SPOKEN WORD

When they took her, it left my heart with a permanent scar.
The day she was booked in - I was too young to assess the loss.
But I grew stronger, tall, and smart, with every visit in momma's arm.
I showed her my dances, school grade advances, and often asked,
When she was coming home . . .

She would say, "Soon . . ."
But sooner kept moving farther away.
At night, I would stare at the moon,
Hoping tomorrow wouldn't leave us the same.
But nothing changed,
Though my faith grew stronger that she would be free one day.
Our bond is magical and filled with laughter.
Love will always conquer hate.

So stronger I grew, and smarter too!
And on my promises, the sun is still shining.
I Love You, Momma . . . and out of nothing,
I've turned my life into something.
But nothing compares to waking up and hugging you every morning.
But that time will come. That time will come. That time will come.

When Momma, comes home-
I want her to take steps at a slower pace;
And be as strong as I am,
And not fall for those traps that separates us.
I want her to feel "beautiful,"
After being caged in such a dirty place.
She deserves better!
And I'll be here to help her to feel special,
Just the way she was made.
When Momma comes home.

"That Invisible Door"

Written by Pariah/ Robert Cooper

"PIECES OF A GIANT"

SPOKEN WORD

Tear drops from a tier,
Falls heavy down below!
I'm so close to Tupac's struggles,
I can feel his pulse.
I'm an unfinished portrait of despair chasing God.
I can paint "Tulsa Massacre" with words in the dark.
I'm jaded and paraded through an option of angles.
I'm on the verge of clashing with my detox angels.
In my dreams, I see burnt black power.
Power diminished at the ballot boxes.
Tear drops from a tier,
appear the size of giants in the ocean.
My gentle hands feed lions, yet,
Sometimes my light goes unnoticed.
But still, I can paint you a picture in the dark.
Of Jesus kissing orphans,
And Pariah accepting offerings from a God.

"Pieces of a Giant"

Written By: Pariah/Robert Cooper

"UNRELENTING"

I'm a portrait, Posed in the quiet gazing at the stars.
I pray the God type shines bright,
So I can demonstrate to haters what walking on water is like.
This act is a gesture of picking up your cross and walking a mile.
The world is filled with life,
But no one notices the man down.
But there's no way to ignore these accolades I leave scattered
Along the path, I make up to your Psychic door.
"But boy, nothing comes easy to you even when your gifted."
When failure seemed imminent, I pushed harder than birth did.

Quitters never win.
Losers never think they can.
Winners take hard shots and stay the course.
Even when the bell is not falling in.

Nostalgia?

Come kiss these epic hands.
I can't wait to go to Africa,
To walk on diamonds, and spit prolific gems.

I'm a winner!

Though I still might fall and get back up,
Effortlessly, with no help. "In me, there's no quitting."
And my enemies' venomous envy,
Never seeps into my muscle memory.
While surrounded by smiling hypocrisies reeking with Imperfection;
Still I rise, and thrive in a space,
Where haters utter words that can still hurt you!

I remember all those negative comments.
The unprovoked hate was just the extra dose.
Of motivation that I needed.

The Pariah is lit!

And I'm still talked down on by people I would have given my shirt.
But winners never quit . . . Losers? Never mind them!
Winners step up to the plate and knock it out the park like GIANTS!
Haters . . . Hate feeds the lion.
Bury me under diamonds.
Success knows what the time is . . .

"Unrelenting"

Written By: Pariah/RC

"OH, FREEDOM!"

SPOKEN WORD

Freedom . . .

Awaken he, and let her sing.
Let her show her face.
She's so beautiful.
Make her Queen!
When she sleeps, may the web we weave bound us to her feet,
And forever we see each other as important as the air that we breathe.

"Oh, Freedom"

Written By Pariah/RC

"TEENAGE LOVE"

POEM

I wanna apologize for starting the fire.
Forgive me, for the burning inside.
You still mean more than a lot,
Even though I could not carry the water to put you out.

And, I'm sorry that I hurt you;
The times I mislead you into believing that I was real,
And wanted what you wanted, when I didn't.

It still doesn't mean I loved you any less.
It only meant I wasn't serious.
I still, after all these years gone by, find my thoughts,
Resting on your wings; blooming with happiness,
And blossoming like April Springs.

Dedicated To: April Rena Burney

Written By: Pariah/RC

"MOTHER'S DAY POEM"

POEM

Thanks, for being there for me,
In each and every way:
And for never switching up on me,
Even when the seasons changed.

From April Spring.
Amidst the green leaves,
And the fresh smell of summer rain;
I hold you dear,
Another year,
And you will always be my lady.

Mother's Day Poem

Written By: Pariah/Robert C.

"A THING OF BEAUTI"

POEM

"Oh, beautiful . . .
beautiful,

Are your flakes that fell and changed,
The view outside my window;

A scene sterile and ancient.
Your snow so white!

I can see the crystals dancing.
And racing to the bottom,

To support the sledge of Santa.

"A Thing of Beauti"

Written By Pariah/RC

"NO MAS"

POEM

There's an invisible door.
That I'm hoping you'll walk through.
I feel in my heart,
My wish will come true.
Patiently, I wait for you;
 My dream, my future.
You said you'd be coming.
I waited longer.
I ate breakfast alone,
And again, night turned into morning.
Still, you're not home,
Out with my promises;
Dancing in my tears.

"No Mas"

Written By: Pariah /Robert C.

"PROS AND CONS"

POEM

These walls are the most misunderstood passages of my life.
Within them, are treasures to be found.

Welcome, to where great men are made;
Where souls are molded, and shaped;
And anger is cast away from hearts and minds.

Thoughts of freedom are lost for a minute,
But smiles are never ending;
And stories are being told,
With the clarity of a country song.

"Pros and Cons"

Written By: Pariah/Robert C.

"TRIGGER-HAPPY ECHOES"

It's hotter than volcanoes in the South.
And solutions are encrypted, inside bullets ringing out.
The way we die makes cop's lives not matter.
So, when you fire, we fire and feel a balance in power.
We tried justice, but to be honest, it failed us every time.
A people upset became "Black Lives Matter."
Recorded, cold-blooded murder, and they don't see the obvious.
Through all the chaos, where in this Hell is God at?
Shouldn't I put into question His intent?
He, the Creator, who wanted Trayvon what to death?
They'll even go as far as to say, I wrote this as a hit.
When I sit, lost for words, with thoughts suspended in the air.
I'm expressing, expecting, to get this off my chest,
Because it's enough to suck you under or push me over the edge.
To a movement, I ensue and latch on.
Public enemy number one;
My skin is seen as a "gun."

"Trigger-Happy Echoes"

Written By: Pariah /Robert C.

"THE WEB WE WEAVE"

POEM

Our diversity sends a strong message;
It's unpredictable, entwined, and mystic,

It reflects hope, co-existing with agreeable differences;
While still letting its purpose, and colors be recognized as one.

"The Web We Weave"

Written By: Pariah/RC

"THE PASSIVE PASSENGER"

POEM

I am not the same as I was yesterday, Truly . . .
You shall not find a portrait of who I was before. Truly . . .

The old me I've cast away,
Like grains of sand, watching water carry him back out to sea
I'm in discovery . . .

Seeking a tomorrow greater than my past,
And more rewarding than my present state, calmly searching,
free of Rage, Justice, or Vengeance.

"The Passive Passenger"

Written By: Pariah/Robert Cooper

"ON MEMORIAL DAY"

POEM

As I stood beside his casket, chills engulfed my arms.
I was saddened, then the tears started to form;
But I wiped them before they could caress my cheek.

My mentor is gone
I still can't believe it.
This wound grew larger by morning.

But instead of showing it, in silence, I mourned him.
I'll stay strong, and push on, like a warrior;
A rebel with a cause, not a million can destroy one.

On his face, I could see the crease of his patience.
In his eyes, lay the demise of his haters.
His smile, cascaded a beautiful anger in mind,
His life became a familiar stranger.

"On Memorial Day"

Written By: Pariah/R.C.

"THE WORLD'S GREATEST MOMMA"

POEM

Juanita,

If Momma had a dollar,
She'd give me fifty cents.

She taught me, respecting women was the essence of a man.
As a kid, watching momma carry grocery bags up the steps;
Made me feel like a man, running down to help.

All those lessons Momma gave me, compliment my breath.
I couldn't do life without Momma;

That's why I love her till death . . .

"The World's Greatest Momma"

Written By: Pariah/RC

"THE PREACHER'S CONFESSION"

People say, "You never miss what you have until it's gone. Well, unfortunately, I was ready to put this city behind me and move on, though deep down inside, I remained optimistic. I loved Seattle. I'd moved here from Dallas to advance my writing career, at least that was my half-hearted excuse.

The idea of me moving to Seattle actually formed once I thought I'd fallen in love with a thin cute female, with big eyes and a small, pointed nose. Lisa, it turned out was "Bi" and more attracted to women than men. This revelation angered me, and after a month of us fighting, I eventually moved out.

My co-worker, Randy, made an offer for me to move into his and his girlfriend's garage apartment, which I ended up reluctantly doing. However, this union started off great . . . Then Randy's girlfriend made a pass at me. I thought it best to tell my friend Randy about her behavior, and so I did. And he returned the favor by kicking me out! If there was such a thing as good luck, then surely, I wasn't having any. But still, I trusted that the man standing outside this small motel, homeless, and with $75.00 to his name, would be resolved.

As I opened the office door to the motel and placed my right foot across the threshold, the attendant jumped up from the chair he had been dozing off in, behind the counter, and shouted, "Wait! Stop right there! Son, how can I help you?"

While standing there, still holding the door, I said, "I'd like a room, Sir," speaking as calmly as I possibly could.

"We don't have any rooms." He responded."

"But the sign says that you have two available," I contested with disappointment in my voice.

"The sign is wrong." He replied.

"Yeah, just like everything else in this world," I mumbled, as I let the door swing closed, and slowly walked back to my car. From the driver's Seat, I sat looking inside that motel office window, watching him watch me, and thinking what I apparently knew he was thinking of me, frustrated and angry.

We stared at each other for what seemed like an eternity, questioning one another's soul. In his, nothing registered. As I was backing out of the motel parking lot, I heard that hippie gravel voice of his shout, "Hey, You!" I stopped the car and watched as this gray-headed, short, fragile man, beckoned me inside. I was at that moment, happy, tired, and hopeful. Surprisingly, he even held the door open for me as I stepped in past him. As he made his way back behind the counter, I asked, "So, how about that room, Mr.?

"Silberman is the name," he said with a smile.

"And Yours?"

"Craig Watson," I responded.

"Well, Mr. Silberman, I apologize for staring you down earlier."

"It wasn't polite, Craig."

I smiled, and said as humbly as I could, "But you were staring me down, too."

"No, I was staring at that writers club sticker on your bumper, and those typewriter ribbons lying there on your dashboard, Craig. So, are you a writer?"

"Yes."

"You're too young to still be using a typewriter, don't you think?"

"Well, Mr. Silberman, the ribbons belong to a friend, and the type-writer doesn't care how old you are, nor do the stories that are developed by them."

"So, what meltdown brought you here, Craig?"

"Homelessness, and sleep, Mr. Silberman." Again, I asked, "So, how about that room?"

The room lighting was dim, but the room didn't smell stale, as one might have expected. It had a disinfectant freshness to it. The bath-room was clean. The bed was perfectly made, and it was soft. The room came with a small flat-screen TV and was equipped with a chirping air conditioner, which appeared to be straining to combat the heat. I had no complaints, though. For now, this room was all mine, and I just wanted to enjoy it and be left alone.

It was a few minutes past 12 am, on what we called in Texas, a "Funky Freaky Friday," and here I was fiending for sleep, instead of parties and sex. Five minutes after my head hit the pillow, I felt myself fading off to sleep. Once there, I abruptly tumbled over into a dream that had me free falling from the sky; while an audience, dressed in boots and spikes, shouted my name from below.

I remember seeing platters of food surrounded by thousands of people drinking and laughing while horses sat and ate with silverware. The turbulence was violent; and I recalled being twisted into a knot by the wind, afraid, and falling.

Then came the thump. I thought I'd hit the ground, and had finally killed myself, but then the thump came in twos and threes. I jumped up, my heart racing, and I was sweating, but was happy to be alive. The thump, as it turned out to be was a knock on my door.

"Hello, Craig. Are you alive in there?"

I didn't respond. Instead, I slowly rolled out of bed, walked into the bathroom, ran cold water over a towel, and wiped my face. Out of the peephole, I could see Mr. Silberman standing there, looking like one of

Santa's retired elves. I wondered what he could want, and why now? On the opposite side of the door, I stood clueless . . . shaking my head. Then I reluctantly opened it.

Mr. Silberman wasn't smiling, and neither was I. He had a very odd look of distress on his face, which made me curious more than upset that he was disturbing me at this hour.

Then I thought, maybe what he had to offer was better than the dream, or should I say the nightmare that I was having.

"How can I help you, Mr. Silberman?"

"May I come in Craig?"

"Sure," I replied, as I opened the door wider while making an ushering motion with my hand.

"And, Craig, may I please bring this inside with me?"

"What's inside the bag, Mr. Silberman?"

"Well, just a little medical marijuana, and some personal papers that I didn't feel safe with leaving alone at the office." I looked confused. This all seemed out of place, but lately, I've heard and seen stranger things.

"Okay, as long as when the cops raid the room, the bag is yours," I said, sarcastically.

"That's a deal," Mr. Silberman said with a grin. Then stepped inside Mr. Silberman, immediately taking a seat in one of the two hardwood chairs that occupied the room. He sat his bag beside his feet, went into his pockets, and pulled out a lighter, along with a marijuana joint. He lit it and let it hang from his lips. I looked startled, but I didn't say anything, or attempt to stop him. instead, I asked with crushing politeness, "What do I owe this visit, Mr. Silberman?"

"Craig, I looked you up on the internet. I admire your stories. Each sentence seems as though you're creating a wave that's meant to sweep up the reader and toss them inside this thought-provoking oasis. You have a powerful stroke of the pen, Craig," Mr. Silberman said, and then he took a long drag on the joint and exhaled. I flopped down on the bed and just stared at him.

I wasn't eager to speak so quickly. Something was telling me that Mr. Silberman was a wise man, and from what he'd already told me in his office, he owned this place, which meant he was also a businessman; and they don't usually indulge in meaningless chatter. So why was he here?

"Well, thanks for your observation and beautiful description of my work, Mr. Silberman."

"Craig, please, from here on out, just call me Silberman."

"Sure, if you wish."

"Craig, do you have children?"

"No."

"Listen, Craig, I'm not here to take advantage of your time. However, I feel that we both are in a position to help one another. I'll even go as far as to say that it was fate that brought us together." Mr. Silberman said, with a sense of seriousness.

"Here's the deal Craig," he continued, "I have a story; I want you to write it, and I want it published in your next week's paper. I want to read it in words as plain as they'll be told to you, by me."

"Silberman, I already have stories set for print that are scheduled to appear in the next NewsTalk issue."

"Scratch them, " He said, with authority.

This one will make you famous, and you'll be envied by all your peers; friends, too!"

Suddenly, I thought about Randy and all those other heartless co-workers I despised at the moment for no other reason than the fact that they had stable lives and a permanent roof over their heads. Yet here I was, clearly the better writer, struggling, stuck in this motel room, dealing with this pot-smoking, deranged lunatic.

"But Silberman . . . "

"Listen, Craig! I'll pay you 4,000 dollars on a handshake contract right now!"

"Why?" I quickly asked.

"Because I trust a man who has no friends outside himself." I looked at Ol' Silberman hard, searching for reason in his eyes, and silently questioning his urgency, all while patiently scrambling for words of my own. Then I said, "Silberman?"

"Yes, Craig?"

"Can I have some of what you're smoking?"

Mr. Silberman knew more about me than I knew of him. He knew I was a journalist. He knew I had cleaned out my bank account to pay off the loan on the car I was driving. And he also knew that I was running out of friends. I didn't know his full name, or where he was even from, but this was all about to change.

As I sat in front of my laptop, with Mr. Silberman sitting wide-eyed beside the chipped desk it sat on, Mr. Silberman started his story off by saying he began smoking pot when he was 10 years of age, and that he was born of two alcoholic parents who were abusive. By the time he was entering his teens, his parents had become more violent towards each other, and by all evidence, were paying less attention to him. One night, after cops had brought him home for trespassing, he overheard his parents arguing about placing him in a foster home or sending him off to live with relatives who he knew wanted nothing to do with him. So, on that very same night, he sadly kissed his dog Sam goodbye and ran away.

He was 20 when he saw his mother again. He recalled walking up to the house he grew up in and seeing her sitting there on that shabby porch, with the frame being eaten away by termites, and with her eyes bloodshot red. She barely recognized him and didn't show much excitement in seeing him again.

"Your Father has gone to Heaven, " She would say as if there was a perfect place that exists for such a man. "Sam is, too," She continued.

She never asked how young Silberman was doing or questioned his whereabouts. Instead, she asked her only child for a drink. Silberman felt sorry for her, for how all their lives had turned, he quietly went into his pockets handed his broken mother money, and left.

"Craig?"

"Yes, Silberman?"

"Craig, I am going to reveal to you a secret, but you must not panic."

"Why would I panic?" I replied.

"Because . . . Craig, the truth can be piercing and could inflict self-injury on a person's observation of another, before the facts are laid bare."

"Silberman, I'm a journalist. I've heard it all. So, please relax and fire away," I said, with a smile.

"Thanks, Craig. I murdered my two best friends and buried their bodies up in the hills 33 years ago."

I didn't look up from my laptop, but I wasn't typing those words he had just spoken either. I sighed, cutting through the silence in the room. Then with an air of indifference, I asked, "Where are we going with this, Silberman?"

"We're going along with the plan, Craig. Remember the contract?" he asked. I stood, pointed a finger at Ol' Man Silberman, and in the most convincing voice I could summon, I said, "Silberman, you are going to prison if what you've just revealed to me happens to be true, and end up in the paper."

"Well Craig, I'm going to Hell, too, if I don't confront my demons and get my life right with God."

I just looked at him, shook my head and sat back down. Then, with my arm stretched wide, I asked, "What is your quest, Silberman?"

" To confess and make amends."

"Then why not just go to the authorities in person?"

"Because I'm a coward," he replied, "and this way I can tell the whole truth without it being misconstrued by a bunch of bureaucrats jockeying for election."

"Really?" I said.

Mr. Silberman spoke as if his story would collapse the White House. Before I started typing again, I asked Mr. Silberman, "Are there any more crime scenes that are going to send you to Death Row that I need to know about?" With a witty expression on his face, and a fresh medical marijuana joint hanging from between his lips, he asked, "Do

I need a lawyer?" His question got a chuckle out of me. I thought to myself, "This ol' wise man needs to be psychiatrically hospitalized."

"I'm not a bad person. I did what I had to do, Craig. I didn't even take their share of the armor truck robbery, Craig. I left it to rot, as they did up in the dark hills."

"So, there was a robbery?"

"Yes," he replied, before flicking ashes on the carpet and blowing a thick cloud of smoke into the air. Then, in a relaxed tone, he added, "Four million in cash and gold."

I just leaned back in my chair, folded my arms, and looked off into space.

"You don't believe me, do you, Craig?" Before giving me time to respond, Ol' Silberman reached inside the brown bag and came out with what appeared to be a brick of gold. I couldn't conceal my expression even if I tried.

"Is it real? The words just fell out of my mouth, as I extended my hands out to touch the brick.

"Sure!" Mr. Silberman replied.

I popped up, grabbed my car keys, and commanded Ol' Silberman to stay put, as I went for the door. My friend David, whom the ribbons belong to, worked as a jeweler, and I remembered him leaving his testing kit in my car. I snatched the testing kit up and then rushed back inside. And yes! It was real, pure, uncut, 100 % gold. While sitting there shocked, I suddenly felt a wave of guilt come over me.

This story meant something to Mr. Silberman, and here I was making light of it all. For me, the test results erased all doubts and made the story come alive. And I told myself that from that point on, I would let it breathe, take it seriously, and treat it with no restriction.

Mr. Silberman was from Olympia, Washington. It was there he met Richard and Jack, 40 years ago, in a bar room fistfight. Young Silberman, who was quite stoned at the time, blew a kiss at a huge guy's (with tattoos covering his entire body) girlfriend. That led the guy to go over and lift young Silberman into the air, and then slam him down onto a table that wouldn't break. That's when the two strangers, Richard, and Jack, joined in to help the disadvantaged Silberman. From then on, the three were inseparable. As Mr. Silberman tells it, he was the passive one of the crew, Richard was the wildest of the bunch, but Jack was the wise guy, or the criminal-minded one, who had been sent off to prison twice by the age of 27.

However, this time, which would be the last time, Jack came home with a plan. One he believed, as Silberman put it, would make him rich and keep him out of prison. One which included a well-orchestrated heist, that went foul once he and the crew made it back to the safehouse. At the safehouse, they were to meet up with a guy who went by the name Ed. Ed had a Lebanese look about him, and an Italian accent. He Finally showed up, an hour after Silberman and friends had unloaded the takeout of the truck. He was late and well short on the cash agreed upon for the gold. This caused an argument, that led to Ed being escorted back out to his car by Jack and Richard. Young Silberman was ordered by his comrades to stay inside and keep watch over the gold and money. After five minutes had passed, he heard a woman scream and four gunshots fired simultaneously.

Silberman quickly grabbed his pistol from the table and ran over to the window, where he watched his friends slowly make their way back inside.

"What Just happened?" he remembered asking his friends in an over-whelmed, and stressed voice.

"We had to kill Ed and that girlfriend of his," said Jack. "But guys, no one was supposed to get killed!" Silberman shouted.

"Look, Silberman," Jack yelled back, "You can't put expectations on these things! Stuff happens."

Then came the disturbing cries of a baby, and young Silberman froze. "What's that?" Silberman asked, looking back and forth between his Friends.

"Oh, that's the baby that we haven't decided on what to do with yet," Richard said, with a devilish grin.

Young Silberman stood there stunned, as he felt chills engulf his whole body.

"I had no other alternatives, Craig." Mr. Silberman said, in a tone that carried a charge of emotional pain. "I, at that moment, became responsible for deciding whether that child and I made it out of there alive. So, Craig, I did what I had to do. Today, that little girl's life I saved is 34 years old. I raised her as my daughter. Marlana is educated, happy, and loved. Craig, No one has ever loved me unconditionally, except for my daughter Marlana. It's a hurting method trying to love someone you can't be truthful with, and I've been in pain for a long time," Mr. Silberman said, with moist eyes.

Then, from outside the motel came the sound of a loud horn, followed by a heavy voice calling out Mr. Silberman's full name, "Silberman Canton! I know you're in there." The voice cried out, from a black Ford truck parked in front, near the office. We both rushed to the window and were looking out of it when this large, square-faced, man hopped from the truck and began pressing the office bell violently.

"Excuse me, Craig, I'll be right back." I switched off the lights and stood there in the dark, peeping out the window, as Mr. Silberman approached this man. I saw him hand Ol' Silberman a piece of paper, and Mr. Silberman held it close and appeared to be reading it. Then he tossed it to the ground, and this gesture caused me to become nervous. I thought that I might have to go out there and help Ol' Silberman if things got nasty. Then I thought of that bar room fight he had and smiled. I was very happy to see the man jump back into his truck and speed away into the early morning darkness.

"What was that all about?"

"Oh, just a friend, inquiring for another friend about money," he replied, as he swiped back a pile of sweat from his forehead before lighting up another medical joint and taking a hit.

Four hours later, Mr. Silberman came to me with his request and money; the story he offered was finished. When I re-read it back to him, he responded with, "It sounds like the portrait of a resilient soul." I liked his analogy.

As I lay there in bed with the covers pulled up to my neck, staring at the ceiling, I thought to myself, "What a *helluva* 24 hours it has been." Despite the fact that I had just made close to a month's salary in mere hours, my mind stayed transfixed on Mr. Silberman and his revelation until I fell asleep. Sleep came and it hit me hard, and I didn't protest.

There were no dreams or nightmares to tussle with, and that was okay, but the frightening wails I heard later that morning were decidedly not. When I opened my eyes, I clearly heard a siren and people crying as they passed outside my room door. I got up looked out my window, then slowly opened my door, and was hit by the bright morning sun, along with a sobering group of ladies.

"He's dead." I heard one say. "Who's dead?" I asked, with a ray of compassion. "Mr. Silberman," a tall, medium-built, salt and pepper-headed lady said, as the tears ran down her face like a broken faucet. I overheard another say, "He was our Pastor."

"Pastor?" I said to myself, confused.

After the police investigator had finished questioning everybody, I went back inside. Two hours later, Ol' Silberman's murder had made the news. "Mr. Silberman was and considered a pillar of his community," one reporter had said.

"So why would anyone want to kill him?" I thought. I thought again about the square-faced man, whose description I'd given to the cops, although I stopped short of telling them that Ol' Silberman had spent hours with me. In silence, I sat at the edge of my bed for the longest time, just staring at the floor before I finally stood and took a deep breath. Then, I hesitatingly began packing. This all felt eerie to me. I took my laptop and started to slide it inside its case, and then I stopped. I turned it on and there was that story of his. I strolled down and read some of it, and it occurred to me how I never wanted Mr. Silberman to go to prison.

In fact, I was fascinated by the good deed he'd done, as well as by the courage he showed in saving his daughter, who at the present, had no idea of what he had revealed to me. Plus, I was already visualizing myself recovering that treasure left out in the hills, riding quietly with boots, gloves, and a shovel toward it all. The way I saw it, Mr. Silberman was gone, and how fair would it be for him to not have a chance at defending himself from the readers, or the courts, or whichever came first? Let God judge him now . . .

I pressed delete, and that was that.

"The Preacher's Confession"

Written By: Pariah/Robert Cooper

"SURFING THE COSMOS"

POEM

I'm a writer, expressing expressions;
And a man who despises them is just an expression of themselves.
I'm just the messenger, walking the line of bias,
And in the line of fire,
Keeping an open mind for life.

"Surfing the Cosmos"

Written By: Pariah/RC

"STATE OF NATURE"

POEM

In nature, does God dwell?
Does darkness crave light?
Could water taste bitter to the creek, and the wind see?
What on Earth, does God have in mind?
Where moments eclipse time; and life is a riddle,
Yours, and mine?
Even to God, can nature be obedient,
When its evolution is continuous?
When it adheres to nothing, not even a glance?

"State of Nature"

Written By: Pariah/Robert Cooper

"A SPOKEN MOMENTO"

POEM

I can't afford diamonds that cost thousands,
to show how much I care.
If I could live without my heart, I'd give it to you,
I swear.

But it costs nothing for you to listen,
To these words I often share.
I love you, and I'm thankful for you,
365 days a year.

"A Spoken Momento"

Written By: Pariah/Robert C.

"A PRISON REVOLT"

POEM

I'm broken . . .
But I'm hopeful that I'll one day see some change;
And that this world I now live in,
Will break free from "Masta's" chains;
And be free, literally, and not remain blind breeding slaves,
Working in factories, generating millions,
But denied from being paid.

I'm broken...
But hoping, that help is on the way.
Because I took my labor and resisted, Masta said I was dangerous.
But I'd rather, in today's America,
Fight the fight my ancestors faced, than hang my head,
Engulfed in shame, accepting the same,
And walk away.

"Prison Revolt"

Written By: Pariah/Robert C.

"ABOLITON-MY HUMBLE OPINION"

ESSAY

My name is Robert. Since being incarcerated, I have read quite a few non-supportive and compelling supportive arguments concerning the abolition of prison. And like most prisoners, I long to wail that fresh arm of freedom, but out of fairness to myself, I've attempted to not be biased on this topic. You see, I know from my experience that when an uneducated offender hears that all prisons should be abolished, he or she tends to dispel their crises and lump in their accountabilities with the abolishing of prison.

In my humble opinion: Abolition (in the text that advocates are using) is an interminably complex word to be associating with "Freedom for All" because most advocates do not give us a comprehensive alternative for holding those who break the law accountable. And I whole-heartedly believe that the law should prevail, and yet be compassionate and fair. I find no grief in legally punishing those who have afforded others suffering and loss, yet I put no faith, nor trust, in our justice system, which feels by virtue of imprisonment, they will accomplish a better society.

Moreover, I do not believe the prison abolition fight transcends the problematic. You see, a majority of the incarcerated are seriously damaged mentally. Many of us know no other life outside of the one that led to these confines. And for those here who have embraced change, they may never get the chance to live a free and productive life, given their lengthy sentences.

In my humble opinion, it's highly important for advocates acting on our behalf, to focus on tailoring a plan of action that is fitting and responsive to each group of individual needs, and to rid our system of this one-size-fits-all-all approach. Politicians who are against abolitionist advocates argue with tax-payers that implementing a different module than the one that's currently available to us will be costly, without informing them of the benefits on the backend. And though finding a pathway to freedom should be the ultimate goal, life-skill-building programs should be enshrined in that process.

Most of us who are incarcerated people are not looking for a get-out-of-jail-free card. We just want a fair shot at changing and being productive members on the outside. I envision a time when prisons will be replaced with strong and steadfast treatment facilities that help offenders understand how their core beliefs are the center of their bad decision-making, and empower them with tools, along with a well-trained professional staff to work on changing disruptive behaviors. That is what tomorrow's prisons should perpetuate, and not walls of oppression, or locked gates guarded by men with slave-master attitudes.

It is not of my opinion that we shouldn't abolish all prisons. We need at least one for Lizzy Borden, Ted Bundy, and his boys. Society should note that more than half of these incarcerated souls are coming back to it. Half of them who entered these harsh dwellings were unloved, disturbed, and empty. And if you do not position them in a way that is conducive to their growth, and give them something other than these misfortunes to feed on, then your return will be what you've paid for.

"Abolition, My Humble Opinion"

Written By: Pariah/Robert Cooper

"QUOTABLES"

QUOTABLE #1

Thoughts often blossom into deeds,
Work on making yours positive.
And in your solitude, practice ruling your mind.
Neglecting this supreme task will leave you unguarded,
And preyed on by your own self-delusion.

QUOTABLE #2

Take winning seriously, And keep a practiced memory;
Life is better, when every effort is treasured,
And limits are buried, beneath the desert sand.

QUOTABLE #3

Be strong . . .The weak fight blindly.
Be open-minded, and soar like eagles amidst the clouds.
Knowledge is King.
Acquire it, and make light your journey.
Wisdom will always weather the storm.

Written By: Pariah/RC

"ROSA"

Behind the clouds she sees light, Indicating dawn is near.
Her Stomach carries butterflies,
Done with metamorphous . . .
While she's transitioning to change, longing to be made a larger sum.
Vigoroso, she rose for the day;
With all her achievable thoughts rested.
Straight away her day begins to take shape
With all its concave and convex edges

"Rosa"

Written By: Pariah/Robert Cooper

"BEHOLD THE PROCESS"

SPOKEN WORD

He was a cool kid, whipped up like cool whip.
Likeable, only after you experienced him.
Looked at like a small glass of substance;
But he was more than a drink of water,

Unaccomplished. Yet, more than a promise.
Moreover, his upbringing birthed him the characteristics of a soldier.
A born Hustla, though money at the moment,
He couldn't account for.

Born abstract, like a mummy wrapped in a conscious coma,
He dropped outta' school with plans to graduate from the corner;
Alone, in Juvenile writing Epic Poems home to his momma.

Believing in that song, a change gon' come.
If I fall I'ma land on money. Should I fall in my sleep,
Let me awake conscious of plenty G's.

On a yacht - Enjoying the Caribbean, with nothing but the sea to see.
Endless like the end of me.
I wish a lot of things that happened in the past coulda been different.

But imagine, if I didn't have the courage to latch on to the magic,
And pull myself up outta' the mud in the river,
I wouldn't be looking at the made man in the mirror;
Standing on the outside edges of physical limits.

"Behold the Process"

Written By: Pariah/R Cooper

"IT WAS WRITTEN"

SPOKEN WORD

Most Men come to Prison and turn Muslims.
Others Pick up the Bible,
And try living the lifestyle of the Jews back in Jerusalem.

I choose to keep it real with my conscious;
And with my money and promises keep it 100.

Prison time:
Most men take it for granted.
I use it to throw pen, pencil, and paper tantrums.

I Came, I Conquered, I wrote!
Literally, literarily, I'm a ghost.

"It Was Written"

Written By: Pariah/Robert Cooper

"CHIVALRY"

When the curtain goes down, and the mic becomes muted,
And the crowd has left this venue an awkward silence;

I'll continue holding ON as long as I can to Your powers.
My darling audit audibles;
You're more than a footnote beneath the audience,

Or portal of words unsorted.
In heart, you are always here,
When Not Even a whisper.

Forever my Spoken words . . .

"Chivalry"

Written By: Pariah/RC

Milton Keynes UK
Ingram Content Group UK Ltd.
UKHW020628180923
428890UK00014B/602